Elephant in the Dark

Elephant in the Dark

Based on a poem by Rumi

Retold by Mina Javaherbin

Pictures by Eugene Yelchin

Scholastic Press ◆ New York

To my sister,
Maryam

— M.J.

To my boys,
Isaac and Ezra

— E.Y.

Merchant Ahmad had brought a mysterious creature all the way from India!

The news spread fast through the village.
What could the huge beast be?

The villagers ran to the merchant's barn next to his house to see this strange creature. But the doors were locked and the merchant, tired from his journey, was sound asleep.

The rowdy crowd woke the merchant.

He stuck his head out of the window and shouted,
"It's too dark in the barn to see anything.
Go home and let me sleep!"

But no one went home.
Instead they decided to see the beast for themselves.

The first villager snuck into the dark barn.
He tripped on a bucket of water and fell on
the animal's long, slithery nose.

This startled the villager
and set him running.

Outside, he gathered himself, puffed his chest,
and said, "The creature is like a snake!"

Next, a short man entered and reached
very slowly into the dark.

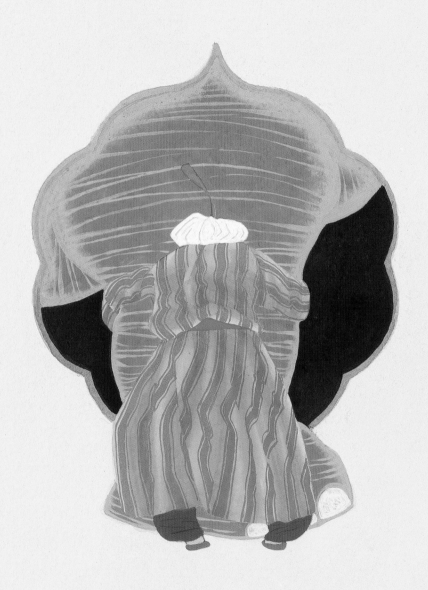

He wrapped his arms around one of the animal's legs,
then rushed out to report.

"People! The creature is not like a snake at all.
Oh no, it's round and tall, like a tree trunk!"

A third villager climbed inside the dark barn.

The beast swept its huge ear against her face,
and the woman ran out.

"The creature is neither like a snake nor a tree trunk," she panted. "It's like a fan! A huge, floppy fan!"

The three villagers argued excitedly.
Others scratched their heads and disagreed.
Each offered such different views!

The fight escalated, and the remaining villagers stole
into the dark barn to find out the truth for themselves.

"It's like a leathery jug of water!"

"It's skinny and hairy, like a paintbrush!"

"It's definitely sharp like a plow!"

"It sounds like a horn!"

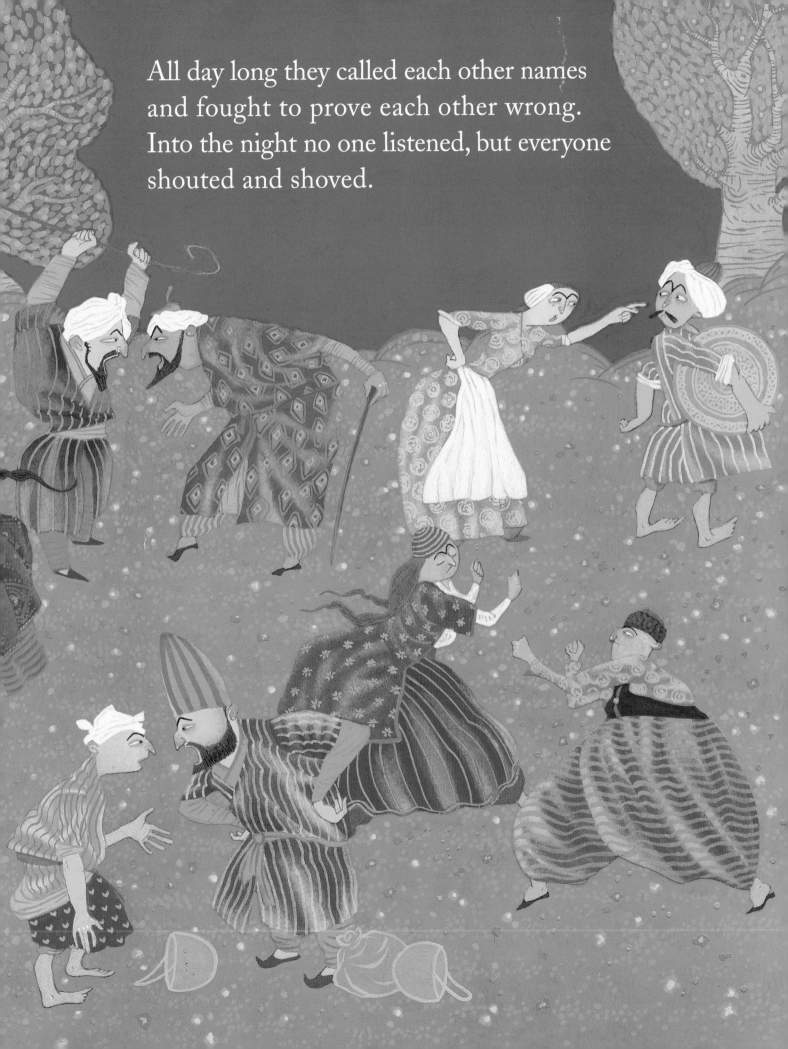

All day long they called each other names
and fought to prove each other wrong.
Into the night no one listened, but everyone
shouted and shoved.

When the sun finally rose the next morning, Merchant Ahmad led the beautiful, gentle creature to the river.

But everyone was still too busy fighting to notice the large gray elephant. And no one noticed that they each knew only a small piece of the truth.

Author's Note

I have always felt a special bond with the poet Rumi. Like Rumi, I was born in Iran (formerly Persia), and my native tongue is Persian. And I, too, am destined to live outside my country of origin with people of many cultures who have widely differing points of view. I often find myself wondering: What would happen if, instead of arguing, people would listen to one another and place their conclusions together like pieces of a puzzle?

In his poem, Rumi clearly illustrates how each person perceives the elephant according to the small part he touches. He also shows how insisting on our own conclusions, made in the dark, keeps us from seeing the whole picture. Further along in this fragment of what is a much longer poem, Rumi writes, "*If each carried a candle in their hands, there would be no disagreement in their statements.*" I think of this story as a lit candle, and I'm grateful for the opportunity to pass it on to you, my dear reader.

Illustrator's Note

I became an artist in Russia during the time when information was routinely obscured or distorted by the government. And that is why I so eagerly embraced the opportunity to illustrate this book. The importance of seeing the complete picture instead of groping for bits and pieces of it in the dark resonated deeply with me. Such personal connection to the story helped me to bridge my art with the art of the Persian miniature painters whom I chose for my inspiration. Each of their meticulous paintings is a world complete in itself where nothing is overlooked or obscured. To make that world accessible to contemporary kids, I relied on my own background in visual storytelling and theatre. In the end, for me, merging the ancient Persian art with my own modern sensibilities is what made the story and pictures take on a life of their own.

Library of Congress Cataloging-in-Publication Data
Javaherbin, Mina, author.
Elephant in the dark / by Mina Javaherbin; illustrated by Eugene Yelchin. — First edition.   pages cm
Summary: In this version of "The Blind Men and the Elephant," based on a poem by Rumi, Persian villagers
try to figure out what strange animal in a dark barn has arrived from India.
ISBN 978-0-545-63670-4 (hardcover : alk. paper)
1. Jalal al-Din Rumi, Maulana, 1207–1273—Adaptations. 2. Blind men and the elephant—Adaptations.
3. Elephants—Folklore—Juvenile fiction. 4. Perception—Juvenile fiction. 5. Folklore—India—Juvenile fiction.
[1. Fables. 2. Elephants—Folklore. 3. Perception—Folklore. 4. Folklore—India. 5. Jalal al-Din Rumi, Maulana,
1207–1273—Adaptations.] I. Jalal al-Din Rumi, Maulana, 1207–1273. II. Yelchin, Eugene, illustrator. III. Title.
PZ8.2.J38El 2015   398.21'0954—dc23   2013049691
10 9 8 7 6 5 4 3 2 1   15 16 17 18 19
Printed in Malaysia 108   First edition, September 2015

The display type was set in Kowalski2 Pro.
The text was set in Adobe Caslon.
The art was created using ink, gouache, and acrylic on watercolor paper.
Book design by Leslie Mechanic

Gracious thanks to Dianne Hess, my editor, whose vision and spirit helped to bring this book to life. —M.J.

This story, most often recognized as "The Blind Men and the Elephant," is very old. For centuries, variations of this story motif have been told and written in many cultures.

For her adaptation of the story, Mina Javaherbin used the original thirteenth century Persian text from "Difference of Opinion/Quarrel Over the Shape of the Elephant" found in *The Mathnawi of Jalalu'ddin Rumi*, edited and annotated by Reynold A. Nicholson. Reissued by Nasrollah Purjavadi. Tehran: Amir Kabir, 1984.

The earliest written version of this story we were able to trace is from *Tripitaka* (known as the *Pali Canon*, Part 2). It was written down around 100 BCE but was known to have existed earlier in the oral Buddhist tradition from about 400 BCE.

We gratefully acknowledge John Renard, PhD, Islamic Studies, professor of theological studies, Saint Louis University, for his thoughtful review of and consultation on the manuscript and art; Amy Landau from the Walters Collection and Karen Van Rossem from the Scholastic Library for their generous help throughout the project; and Anne Pellowski for her amazing help in tracking earlier versions of this story.